I Feel Worried

By Connor Stratton

level
2
little blue
readers

www.littlebluehousebooks.com

Little Blue House is distributed by North Star Editions:
sales@northstareditions.com | 888-417-0195

Produced for Little Blue House by Red Line Editorial.

Photographs ©: Shutterstock Images, cover, 4, 6–7, 10–11, 16–17, 18 (top), 18 (bottom), 20–21, 24 (top left), 24 (top right), 24 (bottom left); iStockphoto, 9, 12 (top), 12 (bottom), 15, 23, 24 (bottom right)

Library of Congress Control Number: 2020913848

ISBN
978-1-64619-300-4 (hardcover)
978-1-64619-318-9 (paperback)
978-1-64619-354-7 (ebook pdf)
978-1-64619-336-3 (hosted ebook)

Printed in the United States of America
Mankato, MN
012021

About the Author

Connor Stratton enjoys writing books for children and watching movies, such as *Inside Out*. He's always trying to understand his feelings better. He lives in Minnesota.

Table of Contents

Why I'm Worried

Sometimes I feel worried.

I worry about going to school because I won't be with my parents.

I worry about going to the doctor.

Getting a shot is scary because it might hurt.

7

Sometimes I go to a new camp.

I don't know anyone there.

I worry I won't make friends.

I worry about my parents. Sometimes they look sad or angry, and I worry I did something wrong.

parents

How It Feels

When I feel worried, my chest starts to hurt. Sometimes I frown too.

I have lots of thoughts when I'm worried.
I think about something bad that could happen.

Sometimes I feel

really worried.

Then it is hard to breathe.

Feeling Better

I talk to people when I feel worried.

Sometimes I talk to my dad.

Sometimes I talk to my teacher.

I tell my mom why
I'm worried.
She tells me feeling
worried is okay.
But I don't need to worry.

My dad gives me a hug
and holds me tight.
I don't feel
worried anymore.

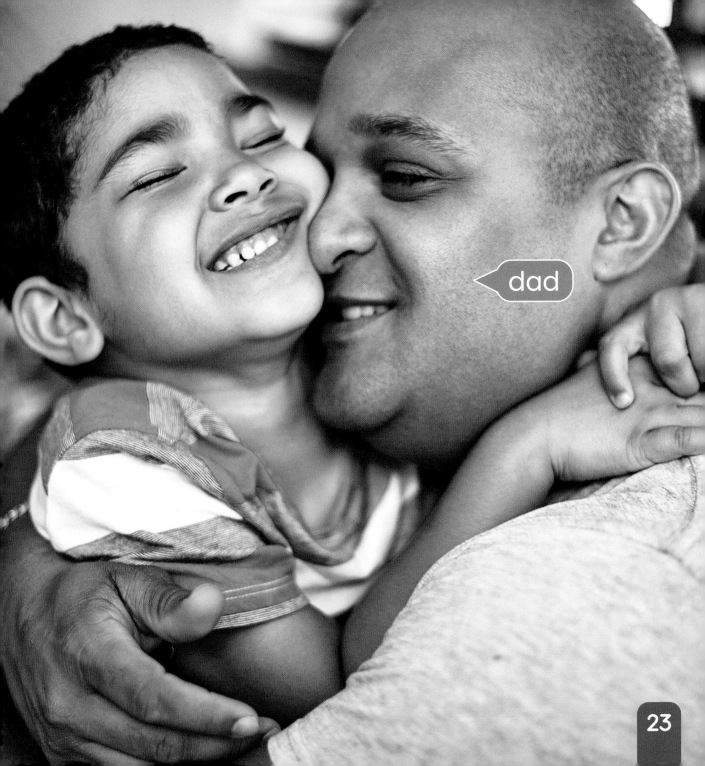

Glossary

dad

mom

frown

shot

Index